THE FIVE SOLAS

THE FIVE SOLAS

THE DELIBERATELY PROTESTANT CHURCH

A. BLAKE WHITE

Cross to Crown Ministries

Colorado Springs

A. Blake White, *The Five Solas*

Published by Cross to Crown Ministries
5210 Centennial Blvd
Colorado Springs, CO 80919
www.crosstocrown.org

Cover design by Daniel Davidson, Colorado Springs, CO
www.bydan.us

Photo credit: ID 83098048 © Miroslav Jacimovic | Dreamstime.com

Printed in the United States of America

ISBN: 978-0-9987863-3-9

To Boaz Owen White.

I pray these truths grip your mind and heart your whole life.

Daddy loves you.

Contents

Introduction

I am writing this booklet in the year 2017, the 500-year anniversary of the Protestant Reformation. It has been a fun year for those who are deliberately Protestant! Conferences and books abound, and we can be thankful for the proliferation of Christ-centered theology in our day.

Now, I am a Baptist, but Baptist history can be traced back to the events of the Protestant Reformation. Before being Baptist, we are Protestant, though many do not know or resonate with that fact. As the German theologian, Dietrich Bonhoeffer, put it years ago, we are living in the land of Protestantism without the Reformation[1]. I am burdened that many, if not most Protestants are ignorant of the significance of what happened 500 years ago. We need to know what we believe

---

1. Dietrich Bonhoeffer, "Protestantism without the Reformation," in *No Rusty Swords: Letters, Lectures and Notes, 1928-1936*, ed. Edwin H. Robertson, trans. Edwin H. Robertson and John Bowden (London: Collins, 1965), 92-118.

and why we believe it. *Christianity Today* did a recent study[2] on Protestant self-awareness and the results showed that 52% of American Protestants believed that faith plus good deeds are needed to get to heaven. About the same percentage thought that we need church traditions and teaching to supplement the Bible. When asked what it meant to be Protestant, 32% said "not Catholic." True, but there is so much more that needs to be said. Only three of ten surveyed said they believed both "faith alone" and "Scripture alone." We'll unpack what those doctrines mean below, but for now just know that means only three out of ten Protestants are recognizably Protestant! We've got work to do.

The plan of this booklet is to take a brief tour of the major events in the life of Martin Luther's journey from Rome, then to summarize the heart of the Protestant Reformation by looking at the Five *Solas*, which were the foundational principles of the Reformation. Before we look at Luther and celebrate his legacy, I need you to know that he was a very flawed man. All of the Reformers were. All people are. In fact, you can see this tension by looking at the posters on my garage walls. Alongside Pistol Pete and Michael Jordan, I have Luther and Calvin. But I also have one of Dirk Willems. He was an Anabaptist who was executed by the Catholic Church for being baptized as a believer. But Calvin and Luther had a strong disdain for

2. http://www.christianitytoday.com/news/2017/august/500-reformation-protestants-catholics-luther-sola-fide-pew.html. Accessed 9/12/17.

the Anabaptists as well, mostly wrongly, though there was a radical wing of Anabaptists that give the rest a bad name. Luther disagreed and criticized some of my heroes of the faith. Again, I am a Baptist, not a Lutheran.

Luther was a rough man. He himself admitted, "Indiscretion is my greatest fault."[3] He would cuss at the devil. He would also pass gas in an effort to drive him away. He would receive hate mail and use it as toilet paper. He drank a lot of German beer, probably too much. His wife ran their private brewery. He could be very harsh with opponents and even allies. Later in life, he wrote some very harsh and ungodly things about the Jews and about the German peasants who were violently rebelling against the Roman Catholic Church. He misunderstood some parts of Scripture. He missed the book of James. He was off on his views of baptism and the Lord's Supper, so much so that the elders of my church would not allow him to join as a member if he were alive today. So, Luther was far from perfect and the Reformation was far from his work alone.

We tend to date the beginning of the Reformation on October 31, 1517, but it really started a couple hundred years earlier. John Wycliffe (1330-1384) lived in England and studied philosophy then biblical studies at Oxford. He refused to comply with papal taxation because the Catholic Church was taking advantage of the people and started preaching on biblical stewardship to a greedy

3. Sometime when you have a few free minutes, Google "Lutheran Insulter" and get a taste of what I mean.

Church. He said God's Word is the ultimate authority. Keep in mind that in the midst of this there were two popes. Wycliffe proclaimed that Jesus Christ is the head of the Church. He preached against the papacy, purgatory, indulgences, praying to saints, celibacy among priests, and transubstantiation, to name a few key Catholic doctrines. He even called the pope the Antichrist! He translated the Latin Vulgate into English and sought to place it into hands of laity rather than merely the clergy. Astonishingly, according to Catholic law, seeking to translate the Bible into a common tongue was a heresy punishable by death. Why would Rome not want people to have access to the Word? In a word, power. They needed to hold control over the people. Wycliffe trained traveling preachers who were called the Lollards, which meant "mumbler," probably referring to their practice of secretly reading the Bible aloud together. He died in 1384 at age 64 from a stroke. The Catholic Church declared him a heretic in 1415 at the Council of Constance. His bones were dug up, burned, and cast into the river. He was known as the "morning star of the Reformation." We still use his English translation at points, for example: "In him was life and the life was the light of men."

John Hus (1369-1415) is another key leader reforming before the Reformation. He lived in Bohemia, which is the modern day Czech Republic. Hus was influenced by the Lollards and read the condemned works of Wycliffe. He preached against the immorality of the church leadership.

He said the pope did not have authority over the Church; rather, Scripture did. He said bread and wine should be served to the people and not just priests, preached against indulgences, and preached in the common language of the people. Rome ordered him to recant, but he refused and was therefore imprisoned. He was given a mock trial in 1415 at the Council of Constance (where they also dealt with the problem of three popes in France and Rome). He was stripped naked, walked past his burning books, and chained to a stake. They gave him one last chance to recant. He said, "What I taught with my lips I will now seal with my blood." Then he was burned to death, singing as he breathed his last breath. He had told the Catholic leaders, "You may roast this Goose (Hus is Czech for *goose*) but 100 years from now a swan will arise whose singing you will not be able to silence." That was 1415. One hundred and two years later, Luther nailed the 95 theses to the church door in Wittenberg. And Luther saw himself as this Hussite swan. Often you will find Lutheran pulpits in the shape of a swan.

The Reformation was not the work of one man or one movement, but God did use Luther in a unique way. He is to be commended and honored for his clarity on the gospel, his courage amidst opposition, and his rock solid confidence in Christ and the Word of God.

Part I

The Reformer

I

LUTHER'S JOURNEY

————————

Martin Luther was born on November 10, 1483, the oldest of 8 siblings. He was a bright student. His dad was a miner who wanted his son to become a lawyer, so he sent him to law school. Smart man. He wanted someone to take care of him when he got old. One day, young Martin was making his way home from law school and got caught in a terrible thunderstorm. He nearly got struck by lightning and fell off his horse. Being a good Catholic boy, he prayed to St. Anne, the mother of Mary and the patron saint for miners. He prayed and made a deal with her. If she would get him through this storm, he'd become a monk. It was as if a bolt from heaven forced him to become a monk.[1] God had plans. He became a committed Augustinian monk, which was the strictest of the orders.

Luther had a terribly guilty conscience. He feared God's judgment, so he was constantly confessing any and all kinds of sins to his priest. Recall that according to their theology, only sins actually confessed were forgiven. Luther said, "I may say that if ever a monk got to heaven by his monkery it was I."[2] His supervisor once told him not to return until he had a sin actually worth confessing. Staupitz, his mentor said, "Look here, if you expect Christ to forgive you, come in with something to forgive—patricide, blasphemy, adultery—instead of all these peccadilloes. . . Man, God is not angry with you. You are angry with God. Don't you know that God commands you to hope."[3] He was finally fed up with Luther's constant confession so he sent him off to be a Bible professor. That's what you do, right? When a man starts losing his mind, make him a college professor.

Luther was 26 years old. In that day, in order to be a professor, students had to master a book of theology known as *The Sentences* by Peter Lombard. That book is no good, but it is full of quotes from Augustine, the 4th-century theologian, who was a much more faithful interpreter of Paul. In fact, one has described the Reformation as Augustine's theology of grace triumphing

1. Michael Reeves, *The Unquenchable Flame* (Nashville: B&H Academic, 2009), 37.
2. Roland Bainton, *Here I Stand* (Nashville: Abingdon, 1950), 34.
3. Ibid., 41.

over Augustine's theology of the Church. His teaching on grace is Protestant at many points but his teaching on the Church is Catholic at many points. The late great theologian B.B. Warfield said that the Reformation was nothing short of the recovery of Augustine's doctrine of salvation.[4]

Letting Luther loose with the Scripture was a move Rome would soon regret. He became a teacher at the University of Wittenberg, a city that was the proud host of some 19,000 relics. A relic was an item you could visit and venerate and thereby shave years off of purgatory. Purgatory is a place Catholic teachers made up where believers go when they die to be "purged" from remaining sin before you can enter heaven. Some Wittenberg relics included a piece of straw from the crib of Jesus, a strand of his beard, a nail from his cross, a crumb from the Last Supper, a twig from Moses' burning bush, some of Mary's hair, and tons of teeth and bones from the Apostles. Venerating each piece would remove 1,900,000 days of purgatory.[5] Luther asked, if the pope has the authority to release a person from purgatory, why wouldn't he, out of love, release everyone? Why limit it to those who observe relics? It was a good question.

Indulgences were what really got Luther fired up. An indulgence was the remission of sin granted by the Catholic Church. Luther saw his people putting trust in

4. B.B. Warfield, "Studies in Tertullian and Augustine" in *The Works of Benjamin B. Warfield* (Grand Rapids: Baker, 1930), 4:130, 131, 411.
5. Reeves, *The Unquenchable Flame*, 41.

these pieces of paper sold by the Roman Catholic Church. If you bought one, you could whittle off years of your time in purgatory or even your loved ones' time there. There was a certain bombastic Catholic leader that Luther despised. His name was John Tetzel and he was a very "successful" salesman of indulgences. He majored in emotional manipulation. You should also know that the Roman Catholic Church needed two billion dollars to build St. Peter's Basilica, which explains the push. Convenient, huh? It's actually a brilliant, though wickedly manipulative, fundraising idea: capitalize on human guilt, which everyone has, plus the superstitious belief that the pope has the power to forgive sins, which can be bought with a price! Need money for buildings? Scare and sell the hell out of ignorant people. Ignorant in the sense that they literally did not know better. At this point, people didn't have access to the Bible, which was only written in Latin. Whatever these corrupt priests would say would be accepted because the people didn't have a clue what they were talking about. Half the time, the church leaders themselves didn't have a clue. The service of the mass was said in Latin as well, and very few lay people knew Latin. A bulk of the priests didn't even know the language. They would just memorize the service sayings. The spiritual ignorance was such that George Buchanan, the Scottish historian, could claim that some priests thought the New Testament was a book recently published by Martin Luther! This helps one understand one of the slogans of the Reformation: *post tenebras lux*—after darkness, light.

Tetzel would go around selling the forgiveness of sins so your time or your loved one's time in purgatory could be reduced. He would say, "When the coin in the coffer rings, a soul from purgatory springs" . . . "Place your penny on the drum, the pearly gates open, and in strolls mum" . . . "Don't you hear the wailing voices of your dead parents. You can save them with a small offering." He would tell them they didn't even have to confess their sins—just pay and you'd be free from purgatory, even if you were guilty of raping the Mother of God. He emotionally manipulated people, asking them if they could hear their loved ones pleading for mercy, begging them to give an offering to relieve their severe punishment and pain. "From this you could redeem us with a small offering and yet you won't." All this got Luther fired up, and one can easily see why.

Meanwhile, Luther was studying the Bible and not seeing anything about indulgences anywhere. Then, in 1510, he visited Rome and was disgusted with what he saw. There was rank immorality among the priests. Rome was the Vegas of its day. Pope Alexander VI had numerous illegitimate children, was known for throwing orgies at the Vatican, and poisoning cardinals he didn't like. His successor, Leo X, was an agnostic![6] Luther climbed up the sacred steps (supposedly the steps Jesus walked transplanted from Jerusalem), got to the top and said to

6. Reeves, *The Unquenchable Flame*, 28.

himself, "Who knows if this is true?" He was disillusioned. He needed to take action.

It was common practice in that day to post papers to the church door to initiate debate. It was like a public bulletin board. So, on October 31, 1517, Luther nails his 95 Theses to the church door at Wittenberg. He was 33 years old. His aim was not so much a huge protest but an invitation to academic debate, mostly focused on indulgences and their abuse. Luther was still thoroughly theologically Catholic at this point. He just had nagging questions he needed resolved. He prefaced the 95 Theses with these words, "Out of love for the truth and the desire to bring it to light."

In God's sweet providence, Johannes Guttenberg had recently invented the printing press. The first printed publication was a papal indulgence, ironically, but soon after the printing press made a way for Luther's ideas to be spread far and wide. Without that, it is likely the Reformation wouldn't have happened how it did. To use modern language, Luther's ideas go viral and Luther gets in trouble. The next year, in 1518, Luther was summoned to appear before a Diet (council) in the city of Augsburg to answer charges of heresy. The heresy was questioning Catholic dogma. Luther refused to recant and declared that the pope and church councils could err but Scripture could not. That was a no-no. The pope excommunicated him in 1521, which meant he damned him. True to form, Luther burned the paper—publicly.

Luther kept studying the Bible in the original languages, thanks to the recent work of the Humanist scholar Desiderius Erasmus. But his major breakthrough did not come until two years after the nailing of the 95 Theses. Here is his recounting:

> Meanwhile, I had already during that year returned to interpret the Psalter anew. I had confidence in the fact that I was more skillful, after I had lectured in the university on St. Paul's epistles to the Romans, to the Galatians, and the one to the Hebrews. I had indeed been captivated with an extraordinary ardor for understanding Paul in the Epistle to the Romans. But up till then it was not the cold blood about the heart, but a single word in Chapter 1, 'In it the righteousness of God is revealed,¬ that had stood in my way. For I hated that word 'righteousness of God,' which, according to the use and custom of all the teachers, I had been taught to understand philosophically regarding the formal or active righteousness, as they called it, with which God is righteous and punishes the unrighteous sinner. Though I lived as a monk without reproach, I felt that I was a sinner before God with an extremely disturbed conscience. I could not believe that he was placated by my satisfaction. I did not love, yes, I hated the righteous God who punishes sinners and secretly, if not blasphemously, certainly murmuring greatly, I was angry with God, and said, 'As if, indeed, it is not enough, that miserable sinners, eternally lost through original sin, are crushed by every kind of calamity by the law of the Decalogue, without having

God add pain to pain by the gospel and also by the gospel threatening us with his righteousness and wrath!' Thus I raged with a fierce and troubled conscience. Nevertheless, I beat importunately upon Paul at that place, most ardently desiring to know what St. Paul wanted. At last, by the mercy of God, meditating day and night, I gave heed to the context of the words, namely 'In it the righteousness of God is revealed, as it is written, 'He who through faith is righteous shall live.' There I began to understand that the righteousness of God is that by which the righteous lives by a gift of God, namely by faith. And this is the meaning: the righteousness of God is revealed by the gospel, namely the passive righteousness with which merciful God justifies us by faith, as it is written, 'He who through faith is righteous shall live.' Here I felt that I was altogether born again and had entered paradise itself through open gates. There a totally other face of the entire Scripture showed itself to me. Thereupon I ran through the Scriptures from memory. I also found in other terms an analogy, as, the work of God, that is, what God does in us, the power of God, with which he makes us strong, the wisdom of God, with which he makes us wise, the strength of God, the salvation of God, the glory of God. And I extolled my sweetest word with a love as great as the hatred with which I had before hated the word 'righteousness of God.' Thus that place in Paul was for me truly the gate to paradise.[7]

7. Martin Luther, "Preface to the Complete Edition of Luther's Latin Writings," in *Martin Luther: Selections from his Writings* ed. John Dillenberger (New York: Anchor Books, 1962), 10-12.

The righteousness of God was not God's judging righteousness, but His saving righteousness—that which results in the gift of an alien righteousness. No one can achieve a right standing, but through faith in Christ, we receive the gift-righteousness that comes from outside of us—from Christ.

More famously, Luther was forced to appear before the Diet at Worms, overseen by Charles V on April 17, 1521, to be examined and charged. Upon arriving, Luther was presented with a pile of his books. He had written around 30 books in three years. He was asked two questions: are these yours and do you recant? In a less known reply, he asked for a day to think it over. Then the next day he showed back up and replied, "Since then Your Majesty and your lordships desire a simple reply, I will give an answer without horns and without teeth. Unless I am convicted by Scripture and plain reason—I do not accept the authority of popes and councils, for they have contradicted each other—my conscience is captive to the Word of God. I cannot and I will not recant anything, for to go against conscience is neither right nor safe. Here I stand, I cannot do otherwise. God help me. Amen."[8]

Now, as they say, it was on. Elector Frederick the Wise, a friend of Luther's, had him kidnapped and sent to a castle in Wartburg in Eisenach, where he went on to translate the Bible into German. The New Testament only took him four months and was published on August 21, 1522.

8. Bainton, *Here I Stand*, 144.

Five thousand copies were sold in the first two months. He finished translating the Old Testament twelve years later. The German Bible may very well have been Luther's noblest achievement.

A convent of nuns got a hold of some of Luther's writing and wanted out of nunning so they snuck out in fish barrels. The leading "Lutherans" married all of them off but one, who Luther ended up marrying in 1525. Her name was Katie Von Bora. Recall that according to Catholicism, priests could not marry. Luther came to see the goodness of marriage and the error of clerical celibacy and said he married in order "to please his father, tease the pope, and vex the devil."[9] He hoped his marriage made the angels laugh and the devils weep. He called marriage the "school of character." They had six children together. His teaching on marriage transformed German culture. Luther died in 1546 in his 60s. His last words were, "We are beggars. This is true."

---

9. Philip Schaff, *History of the Christian Church, Volume VII: History of the Reformation* (Grand Rapids: Eerdmans, 1910), 455.

2

ALWAYS REFORMING

I love Luther, but I am not Lutheran, I am a Baptist. The persecution of my baptist forefathers by the other Reformers demonstrates just how imperfect they were, spiritually and doctrinally.

One of the slogans of the Reformation was "always reforming," meaning the Church must continually return to God's Word and reform in light of its teaching. For example, the Reformation eventually reached Zurich, Switzerland, where the main leader was Uldrich Zwingli, a brilliant teacher. He was in the humanist tradition whose mantra was *ad fontes:* back to the sources. He and his followers were studying the Greek New Testament, but a group of them wanted to go further. One of them, Conrad Grebel, said, "We were listeners to Zwingli's sermons and readers of his writings, but one day we took the Bible itself in hand and were taught better."[1] These "radical reformers," later known as *Anabaptists*,[2] saw no biblical warrant for a state church. They saw no biblical basis for infant baptism. They taught against these doctrines held by other reformers.

Zwingli was close to going with them, but he was too much of a pragmatist. He didn't want to unravel society. He was more concerned with the cultural, political, and economic consequences than jettisoning the unbiblical idea of infant baptism. He blazed a new theological trail and he knew it:

> In this matter of baptism – if I may be pardoned for saying it – I can only conclude that all the doctors have been in error from the time of the apostles. This is a serious and weighty assertion, and I make it with such reluctance that had I not been compelled to do so by contentious spirits, I would have preferred to keep silence. . . . At many points we shall have to tread a different path from that taken

---

1. Fritz Blanke, *Brothers in Christ* trans. Joseph Nordenhaug (Scottsdale, PA: Herald Press, 1961), 14 quoted in William R. Estep, *The Anabaptist Story* (Grand Rapids: Eerdmans, 1996), 20.
2. *Ana* means "again." They didn't choose the name but were slanderously called "rebaptizers." Here I am referring to the evangelical wing of Anabaptists. There were other wings that were heretical and immoral, like those at Münster. For a good overview, see William Estep, *The Anabaptist Story* (Grand Rapids: Eerdmans, 1996) and Leonard Verduin, *The Reformers and their Stepchildren* (Grand Rapids: Eerdmans, 1964).

either by ancient or more modern writers or by our own contemporaries.[3]

Zwingli, Luther, and Calvin were working for the reformation of the Church, and the Anabaptists were working for the restoration of the Church to its New Testament model. Their main leader at the time, Conrad Grebel, was given three options: submit to Zwingli, leave the city, or be imprisoned. He chose prison, but before being sentenced the Anabaptists made a move. On January 21, 1525, a group of about a dozen men met in the home of Felix Manz. A former priest named George Blaurock was first baptized by Conrad, then George baptized the rest of the group. The free church was born.

We take religious liberty for granted today, but we owe it to these men and women of God. And we should be rebuked by their courage. They were persecuted, by Catholics and Protestants, for their beliefs about a Church only consisting of believers. They saw it as a matter of protecting the purity of the Church of the Lord Jesus Christ. I think they were right.

In the chapters ahead, we will take a look at the foundational truths on which there is agreement among all deliberate Protestants: the five *solas*.

3. Ulrich Zwingli, "Of Baptism," in *Zwingli and Bullinger*, Library of Christian Classics, vol. 24, trans. G.W. Bromiley (Philadelphia: Westminster, 1953), 130.

Part II

The Five Solas

All this begs the question, "Were the Reformers right?" "Is any of this relevant today?" "Are we still protesting?" As we'll see, yes, but first let me mention the commonalities between historic Catholics and Protestants. We both affirm the doctrine of the Trinity, the nature of God as one, as creator, as personal, the divinity of Jesus Christ, the person of the Holy Spirit, the glory and travesty of human beings, the physical second coming of Jesus Christ, the resurrection of Christ and the resurrection of the dead, and the reality of final judgement. These are no small things. In fact, here in America there are as many theologically liberal Protestants as Catholics, and it may be safe to say that we have more in common with Rome than with many liberal Protestants that dismiss key parts of Scripture and deny or redefine historic Christian doctrines.

But there are significant differences and they are best

summarized by the five *solas*, which means the five alones: Scripture alone, Christ alone, faith alone, grace alone, and the glory of God alone. These are glorious truths. Believe it or not, I had these *solas* on the groom's cake at my wedding in 2006. They get to the heart of the gospel and the Christian faith.

3

SCRIPTURE ALONE
_____

The first *sola* we will look at is the main one because the differences between Rome and Protestants boil down to the issue of authority. What is our ultimate authority? For Protestants, the Bible alone is to be the ultimate source of authority. Sadly, many Protestants themselves have lost sight of this principle and are in need of reform as well. Too many of today's spineless Protestants put as much stock in feelings, reason, experience, therapeutic technique, marketing strategies, entertainment values, and pragmatic principles as they do in the written Word of God. Historic and deliberate Protestants, however, view their ultimate authority in God through His Word. Notice

I said *ultimate*. God has placed other structures of authority in His world: the state, local church elders, church history, parents, teachers, etc., but they are to be judged by the ultimate authority of God's Word.

Rome holds Scripture and tradition on the same level of authority, so that the Church at Rome *is* the authority. Pope Boniface, in his papal bull,[1] *Unam Sanctam,* had this to say in 1302: "Consequently we declare, state, define, and pronounce that it is altogether necessary to salvation for every human creature to be subject to the Roman Pontiff." To be saved you must submit to the pope! Whatever he and the bishops (the magisterium) issue is to be believed by the Church. The Roman Catholic catechism states that the Church does not "derive her certainty about all revealed truths from the holy Scriptures alone. Both Scripture and Tradition must be accepted and honored with equal sentiments of devotion and reference."[2] We, as Protestants, flatly reject that statement.

Of course, when one allows for mere men to make up "truth," you end up with all sorts of teaching that is found nowhere in God's Word. For example, the immaculate conception of Mary (first formulated in the mid-1800's) and her perpetual virginity have no biblical basis whatsoever.[3] The celibacy of the priesthood is also scripturally unsound because Peter, supposedly the first

---

1. *Bulla* means seal
2. Catechism of the Catholic Church (New York: Doubleday, 1995), 31.
3. In the 1950s, they began teaching that she ascended bodily into heaven and didn't see the grave.

pope, was married. Their teachers made up different kinds of sins, mortal and venial, which are not found in Scripture. Another Catholic invention is the doctrine of *transubstantiation*, where the elements of communion literally become the body and blood of Jesus as the priest says "*hoc est corpus meum*" (Latin for "this is my body").[4] Purgatory—the place between earth and heaven where we are purged of the sins that Christ did not fully atone for until we are made fit for heaven—is not taught in the Bible. Nor is their teaching on indulgences, by which a person's sins are remitted so that they spend less time in purgatory. As mentioned, in Luther's day, indulgences were purchased, giving the rich a significant advantage over the poor, a principle that is the opposite of what our Lord taught and modeled. A few years ago, the pope granted indulgences to Catholics who followed him on Twitter. (Yes, I am serious.) We could keep going but won't.

For Protestants, if a doctrine is not found in the Bible, it is not to be believed. Luther said, "No Christian believer can be forced beyond Holy Scripture." In another place he wrote, "What is asserted without the Scriptures or proven revelation may be held as an opinion, but need not be believed."[5] Luther also said, "As for me, I pit against the dicta of the fathers, of men, of angels, of demons, not ancient usage, not the great mass of people, but solely the

4. From this phrase we derive the term "hocus pocus."
5. *Luther's Works, Volume 36: Word and Sacrament II*, ed. Abdel Ross Wentz (Philadelphia: Muhlenberg, 1959), 29.

Word of eternal majesty, the Gospel . . . . Here I stand; here I sit; here I stay; here I glory; here I triumph; here I scorn papists, Thomists, Henricists, sophists, and all the gates of hell, to say nothing of the words of men, however holy, or of deceptive usage. God's Word is above all."[6] That's the Protestant view.

Many places in Scripture establish the Protestant view. Second Timothy 3:16 reads, "All Scripture is breathed out by God and profitable for teaching, for reproof, for correction, and for training in righteousness." Scripture, unlike tradition, is God-breathed. It is from Him. Scripture is God's Word written and therefore authoritative. The nature of God's Word necessitates that it is the ultimate and final authority.

Second Peter 1:19-21 says, "And we have the prophetic word more fully confirmed, to which you will do well to pay attention as to a lamp shining in a dark place, until the day dawns and the morning star rises in your hearts, knowing this first of all, that no prophecy of Scripture comes from someone's own interpretation. For no prophecy was ever produced by the will of man, but men spoke from God as they were carried along by the Holy Spirit." Putting these passages together, we learn that God the Spirit moved the human authors of Scripture along to write what they wrote so that the result is a God-breathed text. Therefore, it alone is our ultimate and final authority.

We do well to consider the words of our Lord to those

6. Ewald M. Plass, *What Luther Says* (Saint Louis: Concordia, 1959), 1368.

who would elevate tradition over the Word of God. He told the Jewish leaders, "You leave the commandment of God and hold to the tradition of men. . . . You have a fine way of rejecting the commandment of God in order to establish your tradition (Mark 7:8-9). I suggest that we follow the Lord in putting tradition underneath the authority of God's Word.

A thought experiment will help us see if we truly get *sola Scriptura* or not. Imagine an angel comes down right now to where you are reading this, and says in a thundering voice, "What Blake has written and what Luther taught are wrong. You are saved by faith plus works!" What should you say? As shocking as this sounds, you should politely say, "Excuse me, Mr. Angel, you can go to hell!" Because that is exactly what the Apostle Paul instructs us to do. Galatians 1:6-9 says, "I am astonished that you are so quickly deserting him who called you in the grace of Christ and are turning to a different gospel – not that there is another one, but there are some who trouble you and want to distort the gospel of Christ. But even if we or an angel from heaven should preach to you a gospel contrary to the one we preached to you, let him be accursed. As we have said before, so now I say again: If anyone is preaching to you a gospel contrary to the one you received, let him be accursed." In some of his more awakening words, the apostle is saying that the message, the Word is more authoritative than him! The objective message of Christ crucified in the place of sinners to be received by faith is the standard of measurement. Not people. Not even angelic beings. The message found in Scripture is our ultimate authority.

One of the reasons we ought to be zealous for the recovery of the authority of Scripture in our day is because it is the main means God has promised to use to grow His Church. Scripture is sufficient. God works through His Word. Luther, when asked how the Reformation movement happened, responded: "I simply taught, preached, and wrote God's Word; otherwise I did nothing. And while I slept, or drank Wittenberg beer with my friends Philip and Amsdorf, the Word so greatly weakened the papacy that no prince or emperor ever inflicted such losses upon it. I did nothing; the Word did everything."[7] He knew that it was not his leadership, his character, or his persuasiveness, but the Word of God unleashed.

The Word is living and active, sharper than any two-edged sword (Heb. 4:12-13). The people of God do not live by bread alone, but by every word that comes from the mouth of God (Matt. 4:4). Jesus said the Kingdom spreads like a man scatters seed on the ground. While He sleeps, the earth produces by itself—automatically (*automatos* – Mark 4:26-29). God's Word does the work. Which is why the prophet Isaiah says that the Word that goes out from the mouth of God will not return to Him empty, but will

7. *Luther's Works, Volume 51: Sermons I*, ed. Jaroslav Pelikan and Helmut T. Lehmann (Minneapolis: Fortress, 1960), 76-77.

accomplish that which He sent it for (Isa. 55:10-11). Which is why Peter says this Word is the cause of our new birth, that this Word endures forever, that we should long for this milk like an infant longs for milk, and that we grow "by it" (1 Pet. 1:22-2:2).

So, the question is, in this age of rival authorities, do we treasure and esteem God's Word? How many minutes a day do you spend on God's Word in comparison to how many minutes you spend looking at a screen? Scripture and Scripture alone is our final authority. *Sola Scriptura* is the fount from which all the other *solas* flow.

4

CHRIST ALONE

———————

Christ is the theme of Scripture, the pinnacle of God's revelation. To see what I mean, if you mark in your Bible, sometime underline or circle every time *Christ, Lord, Jesus,* or a pronoun referring to Jesus occurs in Ephesians, Philippians, or Colossians. Your pages will be all marked up! Colossians is only four chapters with 95 verses, and Jesus is mentioned 72 times. I recently preached through Colossians and called the series "Jesus Period." He is enough. He is sufficient. He is the image of the invisible God. By Him all things were created. All things were created through Him and for Him. In Him all things hold together.

Isaiah 45 is one of the most explicitly monotheistic passages in the Old Testament. There, Yahweh insists over and over again that there is no God besides Him. "For I am God and there is no other" (Isa. 45:22). In verse 23, He says, "To me every knee shall bow, every tongue shall swear allegiance." Astoundingly, Paul quotes this very passage and applies it to King Jesus. In Philippians 2, Paul says that as a result of the obedient death of Christ, God the Father has highly exalted Him and given Him the name that is above every name so that *at the name of Jesus* every knee will bow and every tongue acknowledge that He is Lord, and all this will redound back to the glory of God the Father. Simply incredible. It is God the Father's will that Jesus Christ be lifted high and given the place of preeminence. It is God's will to be Christ-centered.

We see this in one of the few passages that lays out God's will for history as well. I don't know about you, but I am so thankful that God has disclosed to us the reason for everything. He is not like us impatient parents who simply say, "Because I said so." In Ephesians 1:9-10, He tells us His plan and purpose. With all wisdom and insight He has made "known to us the mystery of his will, according to his purpose, which he set forth in Christ as a plan for the fullness of time, to unite all things in him, things in heaven and things on earth." God's plan, His purpose, His will, is to sum up all things under Jesus Christ.

You need not supplement His person and work. Jesus plus nothing equals everything. To add to Him is to take away from Him. In this case, you subtract by adding. We see this all over the place but very clearly in Galatians. In Galatians 2:21, we read, "I do not nullify the grace of God, for if righteousness were through the law, then Christ died for no purpose." Read that again. If we could gain a right standing with God through obedience—if we added *anything* to the finished work of Jesus, then the whole thing was in vain. The cross would be pointless! But may it never be. He says something similar in Galatians 5:2-4: "Look: I, Paul, say to you that if you accept circumcision, Christ will be of no advantage to you. I testify again to every man who accepts circumcision that he is obligated to keep the whole law. You are severed from Christ, you who would be justified by the law; you have fallen away from grace." If you accept even just circumcision—if you try to supplement Jesus with your own thing, Christ will be of no advantage to you. Then Paul repeats himself and shows that if we try to add to what Jesus has done, since Christ will be rejected, we'd have to keep the whole law. If we seek to sever our flesh to please God in circumcision, we'll be severed from Christ. To add to Jesus is to "fall away from grace." Christ and Christ alone.

Rome teaches that the pope is the Vicar of Christ. *Vicar* comes from *vicarious*, meaning "in the place of." Rome believes the pope stands in the place of Christ, meaning he has the same authority over the Church that Christ does. Roman Catholic priests stand before the congregation as the person of Jesus Christ. But, in the New Testament, every believer is a priest (1 Pet. 2:4-5, 9-10). We all have access to God. There is no need to confess sins to a human priest who absolves and assigns penance and good works. In this regard, Rome seems stuck in the Old Covenant. All the old covenant priests pointed forward to Jesus, our final and great high priest. He is our final, sufficient, and sinless mediator. Hebrews 7:27 is so clear: "He has no need, like those high priests, to offer sacrifices daily, first for his own sins and then for those of the people, since he did this once for all when he offered up himself." He continues, "And every priest stands daily at his service, offering repeatedly the same sacrifices, which can never take away sins. But when Christ had offered for all time a single sacrifice for sins, he sat down at the right hand of God waiting from that time until his enemies should be made a footstool for his feet. For by a single offering he has perfected for all time those who are being sanctified" (Heb. 10:11-14).

Christ Alone is the mantra of Scripture, not *Christ plus Mary*. Catholics elevate Mary to the same level as Jesus, even being considered and called a co-redeemer. But again, King Jesus needs no help. Their teaching downplays the work of Christ. For example, listen to this prayer to Mary that is common in Catholic piety: "O Mother of Perpetual Help, thou art the dispenser of all the gifts which God grants to us miserable sinners . . . Obtain for me, then, the pardon of my sins, love for Jesus, final perseverance, and the grace always to have recourse to thee, O Mother of Perpetual Help."[1] Nowhere in Scripture are we told to pray to Mary. She was a wonderful woman of faith, but she was a sinner just like you and me. She was not free from original sin, not a perpetual virgin, not ascended, and certainly not a co-redeemer.

We don't need the intercession of the saints; we have the intercession of Christ. He "always lives to make intercession" for us. Furthermore, just as all believers are priests, so also all believers are saints according to the New Testament. We venerate Christ, not relics. Though the language used by Catholics is that of veneration and not worship, one wonders if the average Catholic doesn't subtly fall into idolatry. We don't need Christ plus purgatory, no need to purge your own sin. Jesus paid it all. "My sin, oh, the bliss of this glorious thought! My sin, not in part but the whole, is nailed to the cross, and I bear it no more, Praise the Lord."[2] There is therefore now no condemnation for those who are in Christ Jesus (Rom. 8:1). As Jesus told the thief on the cross, *today* you will be with me in paradise, not, you will be with me in a couple thousands of years after you are punished and purged of remaining sins. Christ alone!

He did not say, "It is almost finished, but you need to add some things," or "I have done My part, but it is

---

1. *Devotions in Honor of our Mother of Perpetual Help* published by the Redemptorists quoted in James White, *The Roman Catholic Controversy* (Minneapolis: Bethany House, 1996), 212.
2. Horatio Spafford, *It is Well*, 1876.

insufficient to save, so could you come help Me." Blasphemy! He said, "It is finished." "For there is one God, and there is one mediator between God and men, the man Christ Jesus" (1 Tim. 2:5). Christ Alone!

Protestants love the phrase "the finished work of Christ." There is a whole lot of theology in that little phrase, which is why the author of Hebrews regularly speaks of the "once for all" work of Christ. For example, Hebrews 9:26 says Christ "appeared once for all at the end of the ages to put away sin by the sacrifice of himself." As Luther put it at Heidelberg, "*Crux sola est nostra theologia*" meaning "the cross alone is our theology."

Historically, Protestants have been gospel-centered. We don't move past Christ and His gospel, the good news about Jesus. Tim Keller writes, "All change comes from deepening your understanding of the salvation of Christ and living out of the changes that understanding creates in your heart. Faith in the gospel restructures our motivations, our self-understanding, our identity, and our view of the world. Behavioral compliance to rules without heart-change will be superficial and fleeting. The gospel is therefore not just the ABCs of the Christian life, but the A to Z of the Christian life. Our problems arise largely because we don't continually return to the gospel to work it in and live it out."[3] Luther said, "The Gospel cannot be preached and heard enough, for it cannot be grasped well enough. We preach nothing new; but we are forever and

3. Tim Keller, *Prodigal God* (New York: Dutton, 2008), 118-19.

incessantly preaching about the man called Jesus Christ, true God and man, who died for our sins and was raised from the dead for our justification. But although we are forever preaching and repeating this message, we shall never be able to grasp it sufficiently. In this respect we always remain babes and little children who are just learning to read and are hardly able to form half of a word, nay, scarcely a quarter of a word."[4] Luther's theology of the Christian life can be summed up in two steps: Step 1: *Trust Christ*. Step 2: *See Step 1*.

Jesus is the answer to every question. In today's cultural climate, the main contestant to Christ alone is not Roman Catholicism, but pluralism. Sadly, many of our evangelical churches don't understand this teaching. To see what I mean, go around asking people if God will save the innocent tribesman who has never heard of Jesus. Most will say yes, showing their ignorance of the Bible's teaching. Of course, we know there are *no* innocent tribesmen because there has ever only been one innocent person who has ever existed, the Lord Jesus Christ. Romans 1 is clear that all people know God exists, but they suppress that truth in unrighteousness. So-called "general revelation" is enough to condemn sinful people, but only God's special revelation is sufficient to save. And explicit faith in Jesus Christ is necessary for a person to be saved. Sadly, in later years, even Billy Graham compromised this clear and essential teaching, saying that Christ saves

4. Edward Plass, *What Luther Says* (Saint Louis: Concordia, 1959), 564.

people who may not even know it. Wrong! Jesus said that it is only through Him that anyone comes to the Father (John 14:6). Jesus is the only name, given among men, by which we must be saved (Acts 4:12). The exclusivity of Christ, therefore, fuels missional urgency because people won't hear unless someone preaches. And there will be no preachers unless they are sent. Romans 10:17 says, "So faith comes from hearing, and hearing through the word of Christ." May "Christ Alone" compel us to live lives for Him alone, trust in His sufficiency, and proclaim His necessity.

5

FAITH ALONE

Sola Fide—Faith Alone—gets at the heart of the Protestant Reformation as it is shorthand for justification by faith alone. Justification by faith alone was the centerpiece of the Reformation, and in my mind, it still is. Justification is what made the Reformation the Reformation. John Calvin, another Protestant Reformer, said justification "is the first and keenest subject of controversy between us." He also said that justification by faith alone is the principle hinge on which all true religion turns. Luther said, "Nothing in this article can be given up or compromised, even if heaven and earth and things temporal should be destroyed. This is the article "on which the church stands or falls."[1] A more modern day Reformed theologian, J.I. Packer, wrote, "The doctrine of Justification by faith is like Atlas: it bears a world: it bears a world on its shoulders, the entire evangelical knowledge of saving grace."[2] *Sola Fide* was *the* issue of the Protestant Reformation.

So what is this important doctrine? To be justified means to be declared righteous—sins forgiven and credited with the righteousness of Jesus Christ. It is a declaration. The verb is forensic, not a process. Justification is about our status and standing before God, not what God does within me. We are declared righteous—justified—not on the basis of the process of sanctification, but on the basis of the finished work of Jesus Christ. One can readily see how "faith alone" and "Christ alone" are two ways of asserting the same truth. The key distinction with Rome is that in the New Testament to be justified is not to be made righteous, but to be declared righteous.

Protestants have guarded the truth of faith alone by distinguishing between justification and sanctification. Justification is a one-time declaration that we are right with God. Sanctification is the ongoing process of growing in conformity to Christ. Justification is being declared righteous. Sanctification is being made righteous. Justification is a position before God. Sanctification is our

1. Martin Brecht, *Martin Luther: The Preservation of the Church, 1532-1546, Volume 3* (Minneapolis: Fortress Press, 1999), 180.
2. J.I. Packer, "Introductory Essay," in the Banner of Truth edition of James Buchanah's *The Doctrine of Justification*, viii.

practice of godliness. Justification is immediate. Sanctification is a process. Justification is objective. Sanctification is subjective.[3] Justification is the basis of sanctification, but according to Rome, justification and sanctification are the same thing. So, your standing with God is dependent on your holiness. And you can lose your justification. Here is how Pope John Paul II put it in the catechism: Justification is "not only the remission of sins but also the sanctification and renewal of the inner man." But this just flat contradicts the New Testament and the very definition of the word. Justification is a pronouncement, not a process. You cannot lose it. The opposite of justification is condemnation, and for those in Christ there is therefore *now no* condemnation because of what Christ has done on our behalf (Rom. 8:1).

Sola Fide leads to assurance, which is a blessed thing for Protestants, but a bad thing according to Rome. Catholic theologian Ludwig Ott writes, "The reason for the uncertainty of the state of grace lies in this, that without a special revelation nobody can with certainty of faith know whether or not he has fulfilled all the conditions which are necessary for achieving justification."[4] Catholics do not know whether or not their works are sufficient to save themselves. Catholics think Protestants are presumptuous and arrogant to say we know we are saved, and we would

3. C.J. Mahaney, *Living the Cross Centered Life* (Colorado Springs: Multnomah, 2006), 118.
4. Ludwig Ott, *Fundamentals of Catholic Dogma* (Rockford, Ill: TAN Books and Publishers, 1974), 262.

be if we said it was because of us, but we don't. We have assurance, blessed assurance, because of the finished work of Christ. We are assured not because of what we do but because of what Christ has done in our place.

Protestants believe that justification is by faith alone. Rome teaches justification by faith plus works. Faith plus penance, plus baptism, and plus being a part of the Roman Catholic Church. They don't view us as a true church. For most of their history they viewed us as damned, but Vatican II softened the language they use to refer to non-Catholics. Vatican II contradicts the rest of historic Catholic doctrine, which insisted that no one can be saved apart from the Roman Catholic Church.

However, most Catholics do not know that they believe Protestants are damned to hell, which makes for interesting conversations when I tell them their doctrine. Listen to the Council of Trent, the 19th Ecumenical Council, and note that if a person is Catholic, this is what they believe. To be Catholic is to believe this dogma: "If anyone says that the sinner is justified by faith alone, meaning that nothing else is required to cooperate in order to obtain the grace of justification, and that it is not in any way necessary that he be prepared and disposed by the action of his own will, let him be anathema" (Canon 9). In other words, if one believes that works are not necessary for justification, they are eternally condemned. Canon 12 states, "If anyone says that justifying faith is nothing else than confidence in divine mercy, which remits sins for

Christ's sake, or that it is this confidence alone that justifies us, let him be anathema." So if you believe in faith alone, you are condemned by Rome. Canon 30 states, "If anyone says that after the reception of the grace of justification the guilt is so remitted and the debt of eternal punishment so blotted out to every repentant sinner, that no debt of temporal punishment remains to be discharged either in this world or in purgatory before the gates of heaven can be opened, let him be anathema." In other words, if you do not believe in purgatory, you are damned to hell!

What is tragically ironic is the context from which they pull the language "let them be anathema." Galatians 1:6-8 says, "I am astonished that you are so quickly deserting him who called you in the grace of Christ and are turning to a different gospel – not that there is another one, but there are some who trouble you and want to distort the gospel of Christ. But even if we or an angel from heaven should preach to you a gospel contrary to the one we preached to you, let him be accursed." Here, Paul is saying that anyone who departs from the received gospel is accursed. And just in case, for some reason, we missed it, Paul repeats himself in the next verse: "As we have said before, so now I say again: If anyone is preaching to you a gospel contrary to the one you received, let him be accursed."

Paul goes on to define the gospel in terms of justification

by faith, not works. Notice that he says the same thing three times in Galatians 2:16:

1. "we know that a person is not justified by works of the law but through faith in Jesus Christ,

2. so we also have believed in Christ Jesus, in order to be justified by faith in Christ and not by works of the law,

3. because by works of the law no one will be justified."

So the fact that Rome uses language from Galatians to teach the opposite of what Galatians teaches is frightening indeed.

Romans 3:19-24 is crystal clear as well:

"Now we know that whatever the law says it speaks to those who are under the law, so that every mouth may be stopped, and the whole world may be held accountable to God. For by works of the law no human being will be justified in his sight, since through the law comes knowledge of sin. But now the righteousness of God has been manifested apart from the law, although the Law and the Prophets bear witness to it— the righteousness of God through faith in Jesus Christ for all who believe. For there is no distinction: for all have sinned and fall short of the glory of God, and are justified by his grace as a gift, through the redemption that is in Christ Jesus."

The goal of the law is to "stop mouths" because by it no person will be justified. Justification is not by works.

But, God's justifying activity, His "righteousness" is now revealed apart from the law. The law does not lead to righteousness. It was never God's intention for it to do so (Gal. 3:16-24). But the Old Testament did prophesy about this coming gift of righteousness. This gift is given through faith in Jesus for all who believe. Notice the emphasis. Through *faith* for all who *believe*. It must be a gift because we have all sinned and are justified by His grace as a gift through Christ's redemption.

Then in the next chapter, we find yet more teaching on *sola fide*. Romans 4:4-5 says, "Now to the one who works, his wages are not counted as a gift but as his due. And to the one who does not work but believes in him who justifies the ungodly, his faith is counted as righteousness." If we work, we are owed. It is a wage, not a gift. But for the one who works not, it is a gift. We do not work for righteousness, but we believe in Christ for the right standing we ungodly sinners so desperately need. Here is how Luther put it at the Heidelberg Disputation: "He is not righteous who does much, but he who, without work, believes much in Christ." God donates what He demands. We depend not on our merits, but His. He requires perfect righteousness, and He grants what He requires: the righteousness of Christ. The Reformers spoke of the gift of an alien righteousness, not because it is from outer space, but because it comes from outside of us. As Philippians 3:9 says, we want to "be found in him, not having a righteousness of my own that comes from the law, but that which comes through faith in Christ, the righteousness from God that depends on faith." It is the "from-God-not-from-us" righteousness we need.

This is what distinguishes Protestant Christianity from Catholicism and indeed from every other religion. Tim Keller writes, "Religion operates on the principle of 'I obey—therefore I am accepted by God.' The basic operating principle of the gospel is 'I am accepted by God through the work of Jesus Christ—therefore I obey'."[5] And this makes a huge practical difference in how we live and think. Joy is at stake. Comfort is at stake. Assurance is at stake. Hope is at stake. Every time you sin, you create a reason to doubt God's acceptance of you. Where will you turn? To your own pitiful penance and worthless works or to the cross of Christ where your debt was paid in full?

Faith alone is the heart of the gospel, which is why so many of the classic hymns are focused on this truth:

- "My hope is built on nothing less, Than Jesus' blood and righteousness; I dare not trust the sweetest frame, But wholly lean on Jesus' name. On Christ, the solid Rock, I stand; All other ground is sinking sand . . . . When He shall come with trumpet sound, Oh, may I then in Him be found, Clothed in His righteousness alone, Faultless to stand before the throne!"[6]

5. Tim Keller, *The Prodigal God* (New York: Dutton, 2008), 114.
6. Edward Mote, "My Hope is Built on Nothing Less."

- "Jesus paid it all, All to Him I owe; Sin had left a crimson stain, He washed it white as snow. For nothing good have I, Whereby Thy grace to claim; I'll wash my garments white In the blood of Calv'ry's Lamb. And now complete in Him, My robe, His righteousness, Close sheltered 'neath His side, I am divinely blest."[7]

- "I will not boast in anything, No gifts, no power, no wisdom, But I will boast in Jesus Christ His death and resurrection. Why should I gain from His reward? I cannot give an answer. But this I know with all my heart, His wounds have paid my ransom."[8]

- "Nothing can for sin atone, Nothing but the blood of Jesus. Naught of good that I have done, Nothing but the blood of Jesus. This is all my hope and peace, Nothing but the blood of Jesus; This is all my righteousness, Nothing but the blood of Jesus."[9]

Brothers and sisters, these are Protestant truths. If not for the Reformation, we would not be singing such gospel-centered hymns. In fact, there wouldn't be much to sing about at all.

7. Elvina Hall, "Jesus Paid it All."
8. Stuart Townend, "How Deep the Father's Love."
9. Robert Lowry, "Nothing but the Blood of Jesus."

Of course, none of this is to downplay the vital importance of works; it is just to insist we put them in the proper order in which God has given them.[10] We must put faith and works on the proper side of the equation. Rome says faith + works = justification. Scripture teaches faith = justification, which yields good works. One cannot improve on Ephesians 2:8-10. There we are explicitly told that we are saved "not by works" but "for works:"

For by grace you have been saved through faith. And this is not your own doing; it is the gift of God, not a result of works, so that no one may boast. For we are his workmanship, created in Christ Jesus for good works, which God prepared beforehand, that we should walk in them.

Faith is the root; works are the fruit. Saving faith yields good works. In fact, after insisting verse after verse that we are not justified by "works" but by faith in Christ, in chapter 5 of Galatians, Paul says all that counts is faith "working" through love (Gal. 5:6). Paul bookends Romans with this truth. His ministry is about bringing the obedience which flows from faith among the nations (Rom. 1:5, 16:26). Here is how Luther put it in his Romans commentary: "Oh, it is a living, busy, active, mighty thing, this faith; and so it is impossible for it not to do good works incessantly. It does not ask whether there are good

---

10. James 2 is a favorite among Catholics. As always, context is key. James is talking about "demon-faith," i.e. mere intellectual assent that does not lead to works. James and Paul are clearly on the same team, standing back to back battling different enemies: Paul, legalists; James, nominal Christians. See any Evangelical commentary for a detailed exposition.

works to do, but before the question rises; it has already done them, and is always at the doing of them."[11]

The Reformation slogan for this idea is that we are justified by faith alone, but that faith is never alone. Its very nature is to go public in good works. The Second London Baptist Confession of Faith summarizes this point nicely:

Faith, thus receiving and resting on Christ and his righteousness, is the alone instrument of justification; yet is not alone in the person justified, but is ever accompanied with all other saving graces, and is no dead faith, but worketh by love.

So works and faith go together, but their divinely given order matters immensely. Saving faith leads to life change. As mentioned above, one way Protestants have sought to safeguard this distinction is by distinguishing justification from sanctification. Justification is the once for all proclamation that sinners are forgiven and declared in the right. Sanctification is the life-long process of becoming more righteous.

Another way of safeguarding the relationship between faith and works is by using grammatical language. The indicative mood declares or states a fact. The imperative mood commands or demands something. "The dog is outside" is an indicative statement. "Take the dog outside" is an imperative statement. Much of the New Testament is structured around this indicative/imperative distinction. The indicative is what God has done for us in Christ.

11. Martin Luther, *Commentary on Romans* (Grand Rapids: Kregel, 1954), xvii.

The imperative is what we must do for God. For example, consider the letter to the Ephesians. Chapters 1-3 is indicative. There, Paul glories in the work of Christ for us and the work of Christ in overcoming fractured humanity. Chapters 4-6 is largely imperative, how we should respond to that glorious work. And the imperative is based on the indicative. Or to put it another way, the imperative flows from and is grounded in the indicative. Which is why Paul begins the second half with that all-important "therefore." After unpacking three chapters of gospel glories, he says "therefore, walk in a manner worthy of your calling." Because of what Christ has done, live this way. The same is true for the book of Romans. Eleven chapters of indicative, then chapter twelve begins, "I appeal to you *therefore*, brothers, by the mercies of God, to present your bodies as a living sacrifice, holy and acceptable to God, which is your spiritual worship" (my italics). Because of all these mercies God has shown you in Christ, live your whole life for Him.

So, we are justified by faith alone, but that faith is never alone. This is an extremely practical doctrine. Let me mention just four ways this matters on the ground level. First, faith alone leads to missional urgency. People will not have faith if no one is sent and no one preaches (Rom. 10:14-17). The means the sovereign God uses to forgive sinners and the means by which God brings us to faith is through the telling of the gospel of Christ crucified. *Sola fide* fuels mission.

Second, the default mode of fallen humanity is self-salvation. That switch must be flipped from default mode to gospel mode on the daily. Our tendency is to think we can earn God's approval through works. We have a bad day and then think God must be displeased with us. We sin and run away from Him rather than to Him. Satan is the accuser. His full-time job is to make the saints doubt their divine approval in Christ. Yet again, Luther is on point:

When the devil throws our sins up to us and declares we deserve death and hell, we ought to speak thus: 'I admit that I deserve death and hell. What of it? Does this mean that I shall be sentenced to eternal damnation? By no means. For I know One who suffered and made a satisfaction in my behalf. His name is Jesus Christ, the Son of God. Where he is, there I shall be also.'[12]

Third, justification by faith frees you. If you think your works earn God's favor, they will be tinged with self-interest. Your works end up being self-focused, but Christ frees us from us. Galatians 5:13-14 says, "For you were called to freedom, brothers. Only do not use your freedom as an opportunity for the flesh, but through love serve one another. For the whole law is fulfilled in one word: 'You shall love your neighbor as yourself'." This verse only makes sense within a Christian worldview. We are free from the law, but we mustn't use this freedom for selfish purposes. Rather, through love, serve—or more

12. Martin Luther, in Theodore G. Tappert, editor, *Luther: Letters of Spiritual Counsel* (Philadelphia, 1955), 86-87.

literally—become slaves of one another (*douleuō*). You are free to give away your freedom, for the sake of the body of Christ. Here is how Luther speaks of this call: "Although the Christian is thus free from all works, he ought in this liberty to empty himself, take upon himself the form of a servant, be made in the likeness of men, be found in human form, and to serve, help and in every way deal with his neighbor as he sees that God through Christ has dealt with and still deals with him. This he should do freely, having regard for nothing but divine approval. . . . I will therefore give myself as a Christ to my neighbor, just as Christ offered himself to me; I will do nothing in this life except what I see is necessary, profitable, and salutary to my neighbor, since through faith I have an abundance of all good things in Christ."[13] Although outside our scope, this is where Luther's doctrine of vocation is so helpful. God doesn't need our works, but our neighbors do, and God has called us to various vocations by which we serve those around us, whether it be preaching or plumbing.[14]

Fourth and finally, justification by faith alone is crucial for the precious doctrine of assurance. Assurance was the heart of the Reformation. Contrary to Rome, God desires that His children be assured. John tells us that assurance is the reason he wrote his gospel! "These are written so that you may believe that Jesus is the Christ, the Son of God,

13. Martin Luther, "The Freedom of the Christian, in *Luther's Works*, 366-367 quoted in David A. Lumpp, "Luther's 'Two Kinds of Righteousness': A Brief Historical Introduction" *Concordia Journal* 23.1 (January 1997), 38.
14. For more on Luther's theology of vocation, see Gene Veith, *God at Work* (Wheaton, IL: Crossway, 2002).

and that by believing you may have life in his name" (John 20:31). The same goes with his first letter: "I write these things to you who believe in the name of the Son of God that you may know that you have eternal life" (1 John 5:13). Rather than being scared to go to bed lest we die and be judged, believers can lay our heads on our pillows secure. "No condemnation now I dread." There is therefore now no condemnation for us in Christ (Rom. 8:1). Any good father wants his children assured of his love, and knowing that we are declared in the right through faith in the finished work of Christ leads us there. One can see why Luther said this precious doctrine "is the head and the cornerstone. It alone begets, nourishes, builds, preserves, and defends the church of God; and without it the church of God cannot exist for one hour."[15]

15. Plass, What Luther Says, 2:704.

6

GRACE ALONE

Grace alone is a natural outflow of faith alone. God owes us nothing . . . . except eternal punishment for our sins, but by grace we receive forgiveness. Grace is *un*merited favor. Or better, de-merited favor! Luther said grace was God's middle name. Grace is "God's wonderful acceptance of us not because we have earned it or deserved it but because he gives it to us freely at Christ's expense."[1]

1. Daniel Montgomery and Timothy Paul Jones, *Proof* (Grand Rapids: Zondervan, 2014), 18.

God's

Riches

At

Christ's

Expense.

The Roman Catholic Church teaches that good works cooperate with grace to merit eternal life. They teach that grace comes through nature, through the water of baptism or the oil of confirmation or bread and wine. This "stuff" brings grace, *ex opera operato* (from the work worked). Rome adds human works to grace, thus nullifying grace. As Romans 11:6 says "If it is by grace, it is no longer on the basis of works; otherwise grace would no longer be grace." Once you try to mingle works with grace, you are no longer talking about grace. You nullify grace. Galatians 2:21 says, "I do not nullify the grace of God, for if righteousness were through the law, then Christ died for no purpose." If we could gain our right standing through our own performance, then not only do we nullify grace, but we are saying that the death of Christ was in vain. May it never be. Let's let grace be grace.

To circle back to the practice of indulgences, Rome teaches they are the remission of sins granted by a priest to a person from the treasury of merit of the saints to reduce time in purgatory. They get nearly every word in that sentence wrong: indulgences, priests, merit, saints, purgatory. There is zero biblical basis for indulgences. In

Scripture, we do not need priests since we have a perfect high priest. The whole book of Hebrews demonstrates this fact. Merit is needed but not from the saints. We need the perfect merit of Jesus Christ. Furthermore, in the New Testament, every believer is a saint, even the jacked-up Christians in Corinth (1 Cor. 1:2)! There is no special class of saints, and there is no treasury of their merit. There is zero teaching in Scripture for the idea of purgatory. Jesus paid for our sin, not in part but the whole.

Catholics are right that we need perfection to enter heaven. Our own merit falls short, being likened to "filthy rags." We need a perfect righteousness, and praise Christ He donates what He demands. Righteousness is not infused into us through nature, but imputed to us by grace through faith. When we trust Christ, our sin is counted as His and His righteousness is counted as ours. We want to be found in Him, not having a right standing from our own obedience, but the gift-righteousness that comes through faith in Christ, the "from-God" righteousness that depends on faith (Phil. 3:9). God made Christ to be sin for us so that in Him we might become the righteousness of God (2 Cor. 5:21). We should not be ashamed of the gospel because it is the power of God for salvation for all who believe, because in the gospel the righteousness that comes from God from faith to faith is revealed (Rom. 1:16-17). Righteousness is counted not to the one who works, but to the one who believes in Jesus (Rom. 4:1-8). Glorious grace!

Biblical grace is 200 proof. It started in eternity. God chose us before He even created (Eph. 1:4, Rom. 9). God "saved us and called us to a holy calling, not because of our works but because of his own purpose and grace, which he gave us in Christ Jesus before the ages began" (2 Tim. 1:9). This is planned grace. Left up to us, we'd never choose Christ. He had to choose us. Outside of Christ, we are dead in sins (Eph. 2:1, Col. 2:13), hostile to God (Eph. 4:17, Col. 1:21), and enemies of God (Rom. 5:10). Jesus said, "No one can come to me unless the Father who sent me draws him." Because of our sin, we only desire sin. We lacked the ability to choose what is best. We were like Lazarus: dead as a doornail until the sovereign all-powerful voice of Christ gives us ears to hear. We only come to Christ because the Spirit draws us to Him. As He did with Lydia, He opens our hearts to respond to the message of Christ (Acts 16:14). We are born again "not of blood nor of the will of the flesh nor of the will of man, but of God" (John 1:13). Through the preaching of the gospel, God grants the gift of faith (Eph. 2:8-9, Phil. 1:29) and repentance (Acts 5:31, 11:18, 2 Tim. 2:25). Grace sees us through. None shall bring a charge against God's elect (Rom. 8:33). He is for us and will ensure that nothing will separate us from the love of Christ (Rom. 8:31-39). Salvation is all of grace. "It depends not on human will or exertion, but on God, who has mercy" (Rom. 9:16). As Spurgeon put it, "From the Word of God I gather that damnation is all of man, from top to bottom, and salvation is all of grace, from first to last. He that perishes chooses to perish; but he that is saved is saved because God has chosen to save him."[2]

As believers in Jesus, we do not get past this amazing grace. It was grace that taught our hearts to fear and grace will see us home. Grace trains us to grow in godliness (Titus 2:12). Second Peter 3:18 commands us to grow in the grace of Jesus. Acts 20:32 says grace is able to build us up. I could go on. Grace doesn't just "get us in;" Grace is for believers their whole life. Our default mode of legalism tries to pull us back into this performance treadmill mindset. We are surrounded by the thought that we are how we perform, and it starts early: stars on the wall, stripes for disobedience, report cards, etc., and we think God's love for us is dependent on how we are doing at the present moment. But we are His children. We are not red-headed step-children whom He is constantly disappointed in. He loves us with a fierce love. And He loves us now. He is not waiting to love some future, improved version of us. I love the image of the father on the sideline of the soccer field. The kid barely gets to touch the ball, but the dad is cheering him on and so proud, just to be his dad. That's our Father.

We have to fight our default mode. We must slay our inner Pharisee. Our world tells us our worth is tied to our performance. But it is not only our culture and our own hearts. We have spiritual enemies that seek to distract us

2. Quoted in John Blanchard, *The Complete Gathered Gold* (Darlington, England: Evangelical Press, 2006), 161.

from relying fully on Christ. There are demonic forces that do not want us to "let grace be grace." As you know, the messages of Colossians and Galatians are very similar. Although addressing different false teachings and even using different vocabulary, both declare that you cannot add to Christ and His grace. The message of both letters is Jesus period. In both letters, Paul mentions the "elemental forces of the world" that seek to cause us to add to Christ rather than rest in His finished work. Galatians 4:3 says we used to be enslaved under these elemental spirits of the world. Then, in Galatians 4:8-10, we read, "Formerly, when you did not know God, you were slaves to those who by nature are not gods. But now that you know God—or rather are known by God—how is it that you are turning back to those weak and miserable forces? Do you wish to be enslaved by them all over again? You are observing special days and months and seasons and years (NIV)!" Before Christ, we were enslaved to demons—those who are by nature not gods. So to go back to the law is to go back to weak and worthless elemental spirits of the world.

Paul uses the same exact phrase twice in Colossians. In 2:8, we read, "See to it that no one takes you captive by philosophy and empty deceit, according to human tradition, according to the elemental spirits of the world, and not according to Christ." Much like in Galatians, Paul is warning the people of God not to be taken captive—enslaved—by adding rules to the gospel. Then in Colossians 2:20-22, we read, "If with Christ you died to the elemental spirits of the world, why, as if you were still alive in the world, do you submit to regulations—'Do not handle, Do not taste, Do not touch' (referring to things that all perish as they are used)—according to human precepts and teachings?" If you died with Christ, and therefore died to the elemental forces, don't go back to their regime by adding these external, man-made rules!

When we mix merit with grace, we inevitably end up with two opposite errors. Luther said we are like a drunk man trying to get on a horse. We overshoot and fall off one side only to try again and end up falling off the other. If we are performing well one day, we'll tend to become independent of God. We become arrogant and self-righteous. "We have earned this!" So we think. Then we'll judge others because self-righteousness always leads to judging others, which is why in Colossians Paul has to warn "let no one judge you or disqualify you" in regard to these extra rules (Col. 2:16-18). This was the point of King Jesus' teaching on the parable of the Pharisee and the tax collector in Luke 18. The self-righteous Pharisee, even amidst a prayer, looks down on others. "I am not like other people . . ." On the other hand, the tax collector knew his own sin and couldn't even look up.

But when we mix merit with grace and are not performing well, it leads to the opposite extreme—depression and discouragement. We sin and think we have to earn God's favor back, and we can't, which leads to despair. This is why we need to be instructed in grace again and again. We need to continually hear the gospel preached. The story is told of Luther, when asked why he preached the gospel every single week, that he replied, "Because every week you come in here like a people who don't know the gospel!" Speaking of the gospel in his commentary on Galatians, he said, "Most necessary it is, therefore, that we should know this article well, teach it unto others, and beat it into their heads continually."[3] We don't move past Christ and His gospel. As quoted above, Tim Keller rightly and repeatedly reminds us, the gospel is not merely the "ABCs" of the Christian faith, but the "A to Z" of the Christian life.

3. Martin Luther, St. Paul's Epistle to the Galatians (Philadelphia: Smith, English & Co., 1860), 206.

GLORY TO GOD ALONE

This final *sola* flows from the other four. If it is human tradition plus what God has said, humans get some glory. If it is Christ plus other things, whether it be Mary, the pope, or priests, then they get some glory. If it is faith plus works, then we get some glory. If it is God's grace plus our merit, we deserve some glory. But if it is only what God has said, faith in what God has done through Christ, unmerited favor, then God—and God alone gets all the glory. He has arranged His world in such a way that no human can boast. The heart behind the other four *solas* is the glory of God. In many ways, this was the goal of the

Reformation: that God, and no other, rightly receives the glory due His name.

The glory of God is His significance. The word connotes something heavy. Something important. Something exceptional. Something with supreme dignity. God is the most substantial being of all. We'll say "that was heavy" about something remarkable, or we'll say they "took us lightly" if we don't think we were taken seriously enough. God is the supreme heavyweight. We are called to glorify Him, to treat Him with ultimate weight and importance. To God alone be ultimate honor. "Not to us, Lord, not to us but to your name be the glory" (Psa. 115:1).

The Church at large has lost sight of the glory of God. David Wells, in his book, *God in the Wasteland*, writes, "The fundamental problem in the evangelical world today is not inadequate technique, insufficient organization, or antiquated music, and those who want to squander the church's resources bandaging these scratches will do nothing to stanch the flow of blood that is spilling from its true wounds. The fundamental problem in the evangelical world today is that God rests too inconsequentially upon the church. His truth is too distant, his grace is too ordinary, his judgment is too benign, his gospel is too easy, and his Christ is too common."[1] He goes on to say, "It is one of the defining marks of Our Time that God is now weightless. I do not mean by this that he is ethereal but rather that he has become unimportant. He rests upon

1. David Wells, *God in the Wasteland* (Grand Rapids: Eerdmans, 1994), 30.

the world so inconsequentially as not to be noticeable. He has lost his saliency for human life. Those who assure the pollsters of their belief in God's existence may nonetheless consider him less interesting than television, his commands less authoritative than their appetites for affluence and influence, his judgment no more awe-inspiring than the evening news, and his truth less compelling than the advertisers' sweet fog of flattery and lies. That is weightlessness."[2]

We exist for God's glory (Isa. 43:7). Speaking of His people, God says, "the people whom I formed for Myself that they might declare My praise" (Isa. 43:21). The Westminster Larger Catechism nails it by beginning with asking what is our chief end? To glorify God and enjoy Him forever.

We exist for God's glory and God's utmost concern is His own glory. The words of Isaiah are clear and worth hearing:

For my name's sake I defer my anger, for the sake of my praise I restrain it for you, that I may not cut you off. Behold, I have refined you, but not as silver; I have tried you in the furnace of affliction. For my own sake, for my own sake, I do it, for how should my name be profaned? My glory I will not give to another (Isa. 48:9-11)

For His name's sake. For His own sake. The God of heaven does not share His glory. We have already mentioned the glorious first chapter of Ephesians where

Paul praises God for all the blessings of redemption in Christ. Ephesians 1:3-14 is one long sentence, and notice what he repeatedly emphasizes: "to the praise of his glorious grace" (Eph. 1:6) . . . . "to the praise of his glory" (1:12) . . . . "to the praise of his glory" (1:14). God saves us for His glory.

One way to appreciate this is by asking whether the cross was for us or for God? The answer is both, but we see the inner logic of the cross from Romans 3:25-26:

[Christ] whom God put forward as a propitiation by his blood, to be received by faith. This was to show God's righteousness, because in his divine forbearance he had passed over former sins. It was to show his righteousness at the present time, so that he might be just and the justifier of the one who has faith in Jesus.

God put His Son forward as a propitiation, a sacrifice that averts the wrath of God. And more *sola fide*—this is to be received by faith. The reason God did this was to show God's righteousness. The reason for the cross in these verses is to show the world that God takes God seriously. He wanted the world to see His righteousness. He wanted all to know that He is righteous. He does not wipe sin under the rug. He does not grade on a curve. The reason for the cross of Christ was to display His holiness. He has passed over many sins and if they were not punished, He could be accused of being unjust. But He is just, so every sin will be punished—whether in eternity in hell or on the cross of Christ. So He is both just and the justifier of the one who has faith in Jesus.

God cares about His glory supremely, which is why the doctrinal section of Romans concludes how it does:

Oh, the depth of the riches and wisdom and knowledge of God! How unsearchable are his judgments and how inscrutable his ways! "For who has known the mind of the Lord, or who has been his counselor?" "Or who has given a gift to him that he might be repaid?" For from him and through him and to him are all things. To him be glory forever. Amen. (Rom. 11:33–36)

He is the source, sustainer, and goal. From, through, and to Him. To Him be glory forever. And toward the end of Romans, the Apostle Paul says that Christ came as a servant to the Jews to show God's truthfulness in confirming His promises to the patriarchs and that the Gentiles might *glorify God* for His mercy (Rom. 15:8-9).

Our lives should be focused on His glory. So many problems in our lives are due to the fact that we are not living for the glory of God. This is the goal of the Reformation. This is the goal of creation. The way we work, live, love, give, parent, marry, and ultimately die should glorify God. Whether we eat or drink or in whatever we do, do all things for the glory of God (1 Cor. 10:31).

Conclusion

In conclusion, is the Reformation over? Short answer: no. Long answer: absolutely no. We are still protesting. To our contemporary culture, our conflicts sound like petty differences over definitions. Sadly, even believers do not like doctrinal precision. But these are the biggest issues of life. How can we know God? What will happen when I die? How can I know? Am I saved by my performance or the performance of the perfect Son who died in my place and grants me the gift of righteousness? These are the most important matters in the world. The Reformation still matters. Scripture alone declares that we are saved by grace alone through faith alone in Christ alone—all to the glory of God alone.

Other Books by A. Blake White:

The Newness of the New Covenant
The Law of Christ: A Theological Proposal
Galatians: A Theological Interpretation
Abide in Him: A Theological Interpretation of John's First Letter
Union with Christ: Last Adam and Seed of Abraham
What Is New Covenant Theology? An Introduction
Theological Foundations for New Covenant Ethics
The Abrahamic Promises in Galatians
Missional Ecclesiology
The Imitation of Jesus
Joyful Unity in the Gospel: The Call of Philippians
God's Chosen People

Other Books by Cross to Crown Ministries:

Exalted by Douglas Goodin
God's Design for Marriage (Premarital Edition) by Douglas Goodin
God's Design for Marriage (Married Edition) by Douglas Goodin
Bitter Truth by Linda R. Graf
Bitter Truth Study Guide by Linda R. Graf
Woman of Grace by Anne Brown

At *Cross to Crown Ministries*, our motivation is simple. We want to encourage believers to live purposefully with explicit devotion to Jesus Christ in every facet of life. This includes Bible study, teaching, marriage, parenting, worship, working, playing, learning, retirement planning, or anything else we do. To accomplish this task we are committed to:

- training pastors who interpret the Word of God from an intentionally Christ-centered perspective

- training elders to shepherd the Lord's people toward intentionally Christ-exalting living

- training lay leaders to direct church ministries according to intentionally Christ-focused purposes

- helping all students of the Scripture to intentionally read the Bible as the story of Jesus Christ

- creating resources that exalt Christ and encourage believers to be intentionally Christ-obsessed in all things

There are several distinct facets to our ministry. The *New Covenant School of Theology* trains pastors, elders, lay leaders, and any interested Christian from the Christ-centered perspectives of New Covenant Theology and Biblical Theology. We also produce resources——written, audio, and video—to help you think and live intentionally Christianly. We hold conferences to bring Christians together for intensive Christ-centered preaching and teaching. We produce music to be used for personal and public worship and edification in the hope that our intentionally Christ-exalting, New Covenant-oriented songs will spur Christians to love and good deeds for His glory and praise. Our website (www.crosstocrown.org) is the one-stop location for all of our ministries and resources.

Made in the USA
San Bernardino, CA
02 January 2020